Table of Contents

S0-BYB-410

As Easy as 1–2–3

1 **Prepare** the assessment task activity.

2 **Administer** the task and record the student's performance.

3 **Reteach** or provide additional practice using the reproducible activity sheet.

Everything You Need

Each assessment task includes:

- **Scripted instructions**
  for administering the assessment task

- **Full-color mats and cards**
  to engage the student in a specific task

- **Class checklist**
  to record each student's performance

- **Reproducible activity sheets**
  for additional skill practice

When to Conduct an Assessment

You may choose to use assessment tasks in any of the following ways:

- Assess students at the beginning of the school year to determine individual student skill levels.

- Administer an assessment after a specific skill has been taught to help confirm mastery or need for further instruction.

- Assess students throughout the year to monitor progress. Use the correlation chart on page 6 to correlate assessments with your lesson plans.

You may also wish to visit www.teaching-standards.com to view how the skills are correlated to your state's standards.

EMC 3025 • Math Assessment Tasks • © Evan-Moor Corp.

Preparing an Assessment Task Activity

Assemble each assessment task activity and place it in an envelope. Store the envelopes in a file box or crate for easy access.

Materials:

- 9" x 12" (23 x 30.5 cm) large manila envelopes
- scissors
- clear tape
- scripted instructions, manipulatives, class checklist, and activity sheet for the specific assessment task

Steps to Follow:

1. Remove and laminate the *scripted instruction page*. Tape it to the front of the envelope.

2. Remove and laminate the *manipulatives* (sorting mats, task cards, etc.). Store cards in a smaller envelope or plastic bag.

3. Reproduce the *class checklist*. Tape it to the back of the envelope.

4. Make multiple copies of the *activity sheet* and store them in the envelope.

Make one copy of the *Individual Student Assessment Checklist* (page 5) for each student in your class. You may wish to keep these checklists in a separate binder so they are easily referenced.

Class Checklist

Scripted Instruction Page

Manipulatives—Mats/Cards

Activity Sheet

How to Conduct an Assessment

- **Be prepared.**

  Preread the scripted instructions. Follow the directions at the top of the script for setting out the cards and mats. Have the class checklist at hand to record the student's responses. Do not ask the student to come to the table until all task materials are in place.

- **Provide a non-threatening atmosphere.**

  The student should complete the task at a quiet, isolated table. Refer to the activity as a "task" or "job," not as a "test."

- **Provide a non-distracting environment.**

  The student should be able to easily focus on the task. Sit next to the student. Communicate in a clear, concise way.

- **Be an unbiased assessor.**

  Do not encourage or discourage or approve or disapprove of the student's responses. Be careful not to use facial expressions that provide feedback.

- **Know when to stop the assessment.**

  Discontinue the assessment activity if it becomes obvious that the student cannot do the task.

- **Be discreet.**

  When recording the student's responses, keep the checklist close to you so it will not distract the student.

What does this mean?

Auditory
Only

Some tasks are auditory only, and are indicated by this icon on the teacher script page. Auditory tasks do not contain mats or task cards.

EMC 3025 • Math Assessment Tasks • © Evan-Moor Corp.

Individual Student Assessment Checklist

Name _____   School Year _____

Skill	Dates Tested	Date Mastered
Unit 1—Number Sense		
Counts in Sequence		
Uses One-to-One Correspondence		
Recognizes and Names Numbers to 10		
Understands the Concept of *Number*		
Knows the Concept of *More Than*		
Knows the Concept of *Less Than*		
Knows the Concept of *Same As*		
Orders Numbers		
Understands Ordinal Numbers		
Adds Concrete Objects		
Subtracts Concrete Objects		
Unit 2—Measurement and Geometry		
Recognizes Shapes		
Matches Shapes		
Follows Directions About Location		
Knows the Concept of *Longer, Shorter*		
Recognizes and Sequences a Day's Events		
Uses Nonstandard Units of Measurement		
Unit 3—Statistics, Data Analysis, and Probability		
Recognizes Patterns		
Extends Patterns		
Analyzes Data		
Unit 4—Algebra and Functions		
Sorts and Regroups Objects by One Attribute		
Groups Objects to Classify		
Discriminates Like and Unlike Objects		

Correlation Chart

School Year _____

Skill	Week	Lesson
Unit 1—Number Sense		
Counts in Sequence		
Uses One-to-One Correspondence		
Recognizes and Names Numbers to 10		
Understands the Concept of *Number*		
Knows the Concept of *More Than*		
Knows the Concept of *Less Than*		
Knows the Concept of *Same As*		
Orders Numbers		
Understands Ordinal Numbers		
Adds Concrete Objects		
Subtracts Concrete Objects		
Unit 2—Measurement and Geometry		
Recognizes Shapes		
Matches Shapes		
Follows Directions About Location		
Knows the Concept of *Longer, Shorter*		
Recognizes and Sequences a Day's Events		
Uses Nonstandard Units of Measurement		
Unit 3—Statistics, Data Analysis, and Probability		
Recognizes Patterns		
Extends Patterns		
Analyzes Data		
Unit 4—Algebra and Functions		
Sorts and Regroups Objects by One Attribute		
Groups Objects to Classify		
Discriminates Like and Unlike Objects		

EMC 3025 • Math Assessment Tasks • © Evan-Moor Corp.

Quick Checks

Unit 1
Number Sense

Objective:
Student counts objects in sequence.

Materials:
Picture Cards, pp. 11 and 13

Class Checklist, p. 15

Activity Sheet, p. 16

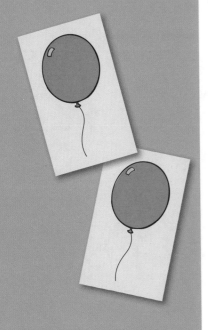

Student Task

(Note: To meet the abilities of each student, you may adjust this task and the number of picture cards you use. You also may apply the task in stages. Each time you use the task, record the response on the class checklist. Write how high the student counts.)

Say:

> Today you are going to count for me.

Place the picture cards in a pile on the table. Say:

> Let's begin. Count these balloons. Count as many as you can.

Let the student take a card from the pile, count it, and place it on the table. Record how high the student counts on the class checklist.

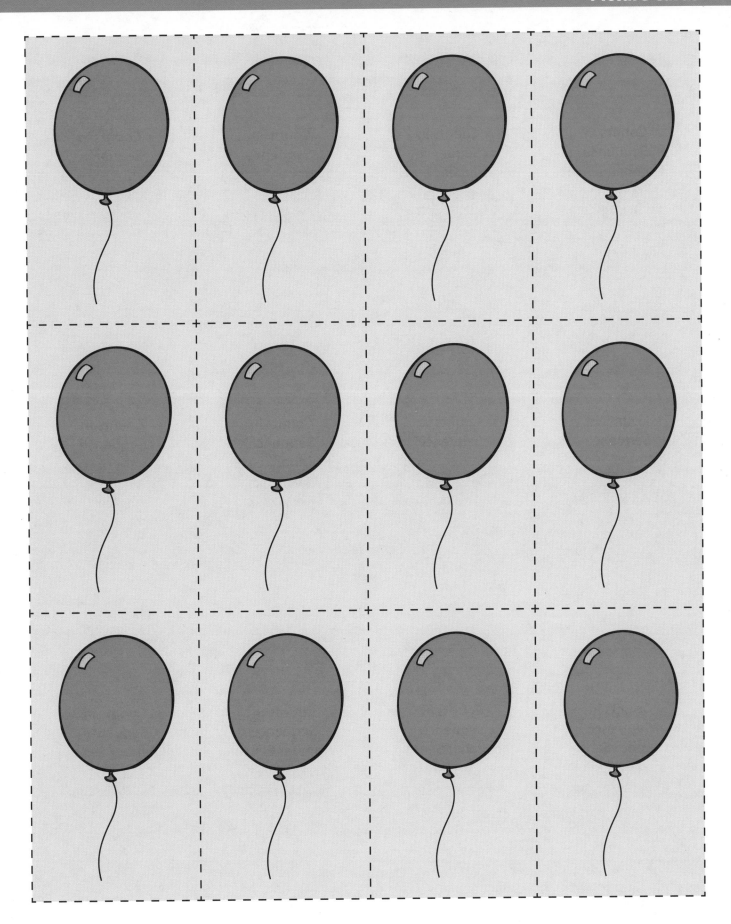

Counts in Sequence

Number Sense

EMC 3025
© Evan-Moor Corp.

Counts in Sequence

Number Sense

EMC 3025
© Evan-Moor Corp.

Counts in Sequence

Number Sense

EMC 3025
© Evan-Moor Corp.

Counts in Sequence

Number Sense

EMC 3025
© Evan-Moor Corp.

Counts in Sequence

Number Sense

EMC 3025
© Evan-Moor Corp.

Counts in Sequence

Number Sense

EMC 3025
© Evan-Moor Corp.

Counts in Sequence

Number Sense

EMC 3025
© Evan-Moor Corp.

Counts in Sequence

Number Sense

EMC 3025
© Evan-Moor Corp.

Counts in Sequence

Number Sense

EMC 3025
© Evan-Moor Corp.

Counts in Sequence

Number Sense

EMC 3025
© Evan-Moor Corp.

Counts in Sequence

Number Sense

EMC 3025
© Evan-Moor Corp.

Counts in Sequence

Number Sense

EMC 3025
© Evan-Moor Corp.

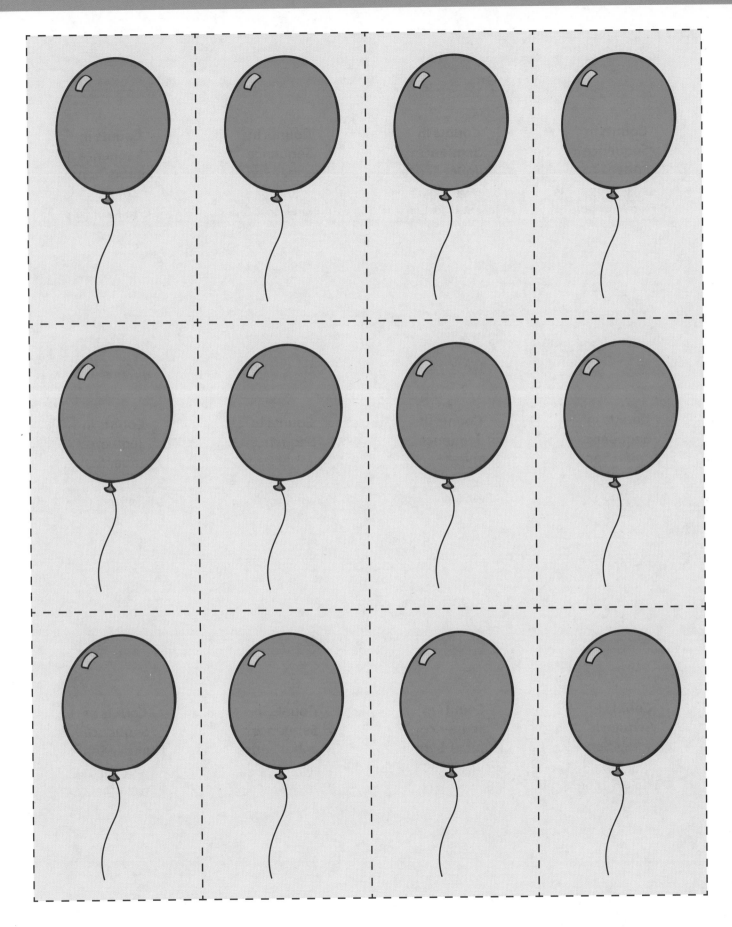

**Counts in
Sequence**
Number Sense

EMC 3025
© Evan-Moor Corp.

**Counts in
Sequence**
Number Sense

EMC 3025
© Evan-Moor Corp.

**Counts in
Sequence**
Number Sense

EMC 3025
© Evan-Moor Corp.

**Counts in
Sequence**
Number Sense

EMC 3025
© Evan-Moor Corp.

**Counts in
Sequence**
Number Sense

EMC 3025
© Evan-Moor Corp.

**Counts in
Sequence**
Number Sense

EMC 3025
© Evan-Moor Corp.

**Counts in
Sequence**
Number Sense

EMC 3025
© Evan-Moor Corp.

**Counts in
Sequence**
Number Sense

EMC 3025
© Evan-Moor Corp.

**Counts in
Sequence**
Number Sense

EMC 3025
© Evan-Moor Corp.

**Counts in
Sequence**
Number Sense

EMC 3025
© Evan-Moor Corp.

**Counts in
Sequence**
Number Sense

EMC 3025
© Evan-Moor Corp.

**Counts in
Sequence**
Number Sense

EMC 3025
© Evan-Moor Corp.

Counts in Sequence

Class Checklist	Write the date. Indicate how high the student counts.			
Name	Assessment 1	Assessment 2	Assessment 3	Notes

Name _____

Puppy's Place

Connect the dots.
Count out loud.
Color the picture.

Uses One-to-One Correspondence

Objective:
Student uses one-to-one correspondence to match two groups of objects.

Materials:
Mat, p. 19

Picture Cards, p. 21

Class Checklist, p. 23

Activity Sheet, p. 24

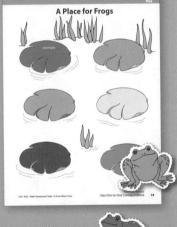

Model the Task

Say:

> Today you will match frogs to lily pads. I will show you what to do.

Spread the picture cards faceup on the table. Place the mat in front of the student. Point to the blue lily pad on the mat. Say:

> I will match the blue frog to the blue lily pad.

Place the blue frog on top of the blue lily pad.

Student Task

Say:

> Now it's your turn. Take a colored frog. Match the colored frog to the colored lily pad.

Student responds. Record the response on the class checklist.

Repeat the procedure and the script modeled above with the four remaining frogs.

A Place for Frogs

example

Number Sense
Uses One-to-One Correspondence

Uses One-to-One Correspondence
Number Sense

EMC 3025 • © Evan-Moor Corp.

EMC 3025 • Math Assessment Tasks • © Evan-Moor Corp.

example

Number Sense
Uses One-to-One Correspondence

Uses One-to-One Correspondence
Number Sense

EMC 3025
© Evan-Moor Corp.

Uses One-to-One Correspondence
Number Sense

EMC 3025
© Evan-Moor Corp.

Uses One-to-One Correspondence
Number Sense

EMC 3025
© Evan-Moor Corp.

Uses One-to-One Correspondence
Number Sense

EMC 3025
© Evan-Moor Corp.

Uses One-to-One Correspondence
Number Sense

EMC 3025
© Evan-Moor Corp.

Uses One-to-One Correspondence
Number Sense

EMC 3025
© Evan-Moor Corp.

Uses One-to-One Correspondence

Class Checklist							
Key:	**+** correct response		**−** incorrect response		● self-corrected		
Name	Date	Orange to Orange	Green to Green	Yellow to Yellow	Purple to Purple	Red to Red	Notes

Name _____

Find My Hat

Draw a line. Match each person to the correct hat.

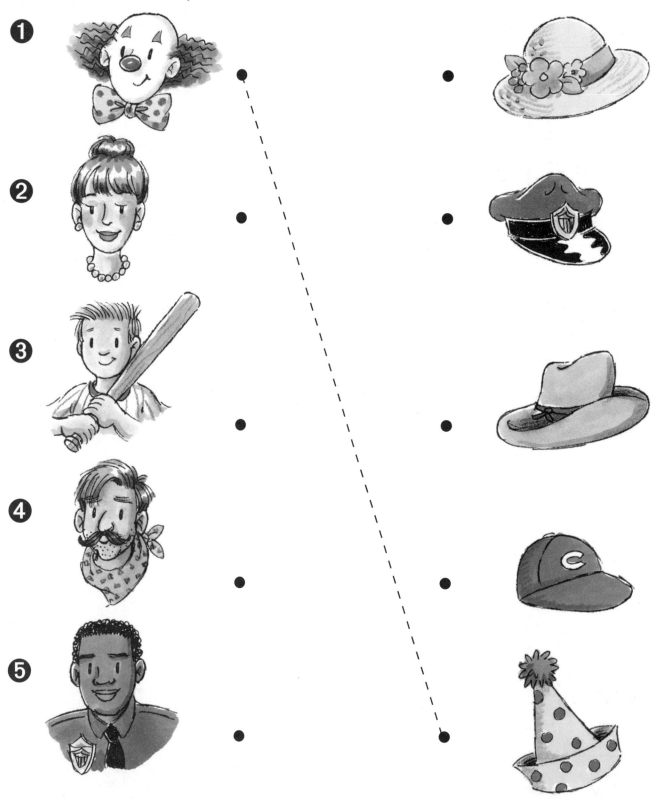

Quick Checks

Objective:

Student recognizes and orally names numbers from 1 to 10.

Materials:

Number Cards, p. 27

Class Checklist, p. 29

Activity Sheet, p. 30

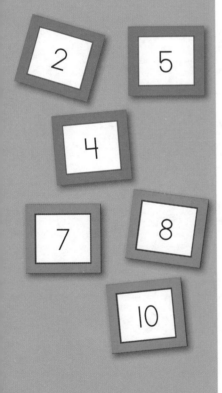

Student Task

(Note: You may adjust this task to meet the abilities of each student. You may, for example, use one set of number cards, both sets, or part of each set. This model uses both sets.)

Say:

> Today you will read numbers.

Mix up the blue set of number cards. Hold the cards and show them to the student one at a time. Say:

> Let's begin. What is this number?

Record the student's response on the class checklist, following the key. Go through each of the four remaining number cards in the blue set. Record each response.

Mix up the red set of number cards. Hold the cards and show them to the student one at a time. Say:

> What is this number?

Record the response. Go through each of the four remaining number cards in the red set. Record each response.

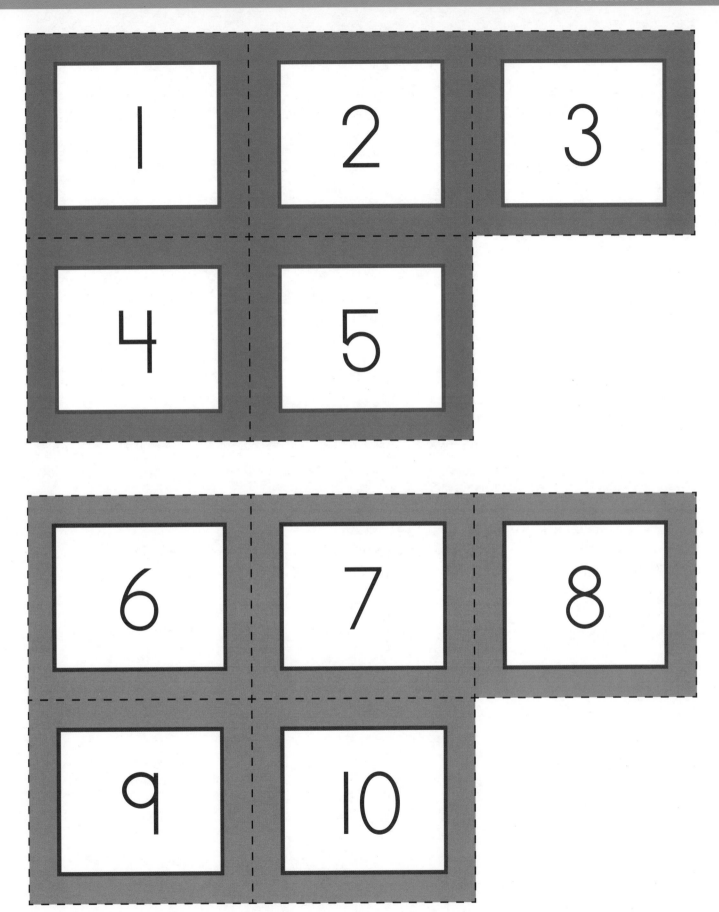

**Recognizes and
Names Numbers to 10**

Number Sense

EMC 3025
© Evan-Moor Corp.

**Recognizes and
Names Numbers to 10**

Number Sense

EMC 3025
© Evan-Moor Corp.

**Recognizes and
Names Numbers to 10**

Number Sense

EMC 3025
© Evan-Moor Corp.

**Recognizes and
Names Numbers to 10**

Number Sense

EMC 3025
© Evan-Moor Corp.

**Recognizes and
Names Numbers to 10**

Number Sense

EMC 3025
© Evan-Moor Corp.

**Recognizes and
Names Numbers to 10**

Number Sense

EMC 3025
© Evan-Moor Corp.

**Recognizes and
Names Numbers to 10**

Number Sense

EMC 3025
© Evan-Moor Corp.

**Recognizes and
Names Numbers to 10**

Number Sense

EMC 3025
© Evan-Moor Corp.

**Recognizes and
Names Numbers to 10**

Number Sense

EMC 3025
© Evan-Moor Corp.

**Recognizes and
Names Numbers to 10**

Number Sense

EMC 3025
© Evan-Moor Corp.

Recognizes and Names Numbers to 10

Class Checklist		Key: + All numbers read correctly. ● List each self-corrected number. List each incorrectly named number.	
Name	Date	Blue Set (1 to 5)	Red Set (6 to 10)

Name _____

I Know Numbers

Read each number out loud.

Hooray for me!

I read each number correctly to _____.

Understands the Concept of *Number*

Objective:

Student matches the number of objects in a set with a written one-digit numeral.

Materials:

Mat, p. 33

Number Cards, p. 35

Class Checklist, p. 37

Activity Sheet, p. 38

Blank sheet of paper

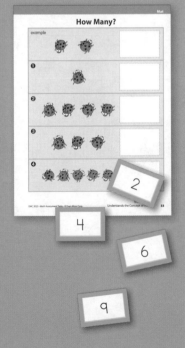

Model the Task

Say:

> Today you will tell me *how many*. I will show you what to do.

Spread the number cards faceup on the table in numerical order. Place the mat in front of the student. Cover all the rows with a blank sheet of paper except the example. Point to the example. Touch each ladybug as you count and say:

> 1, 2. There are two ladybugs. I will put the number 2 on the mat.

Place number card 2 on the mat.

Student Task

Move the paper down the mat to reveal row 1. Point to row 1 and say:

> Now it's your turn. Count the ladybugs.

Pause while student counts. The student may touch the ladybugs while counting. Point to the box in row 1. Say:

> Pick the number that shows *how many* ladybugs. Put the number on the mat.

Student responds. Record the response on the class checklist. You may want to add a note if the student recognizes the correct numeral, but counts out of sequence.

Repeat the procedure and the script modeled above with the three remaining rows. Not all number cards will be used.

How Many?

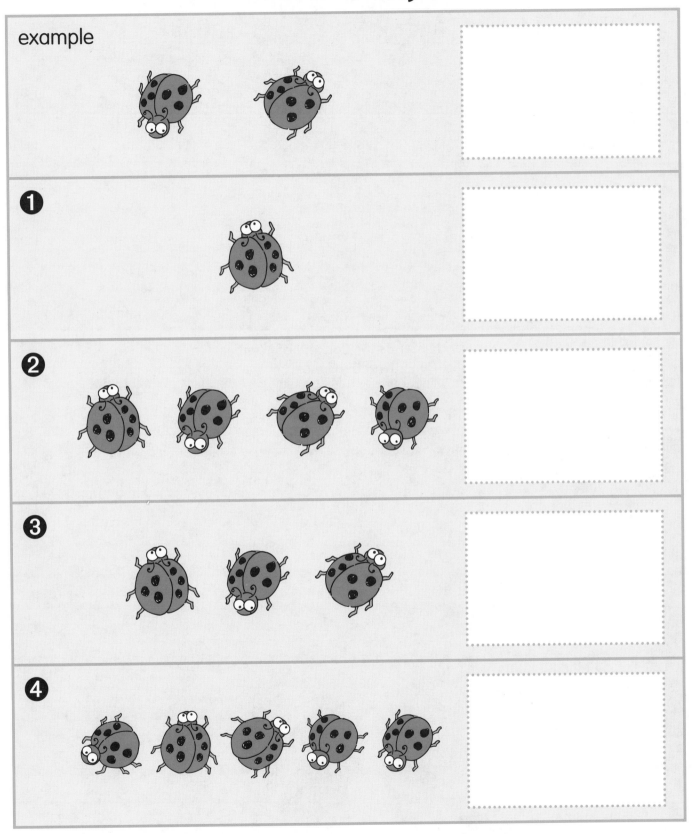

example

1

2

3

4

Understands the Concept of *Number*

Number Sense

EMC 3025 • © Evan-Moor Corp.

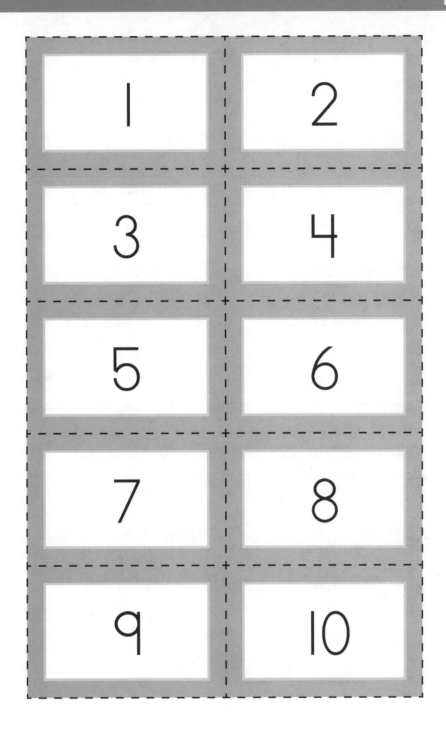

**Understands
the Concept of
*Number***
Number Sense

EMC 3025 • © Evan-Moor Corp.

**Understands
the Concept of
*Number***
Number Sense

EMC 3025 • © Evan-Moor Corp.

**Understands
the Concept of
*Number***
Number Sense

EMC 3025 • © Evan-Moor Corp.

**Understands
the Concept of
*Number***
Number Sense

EMC 3025 • © Evan-Moor Corp.

**Understands
the Concept of
*Number***
Number Sense

EMC 3025 • © Evan-Moor Corp.

**Understands
the Concept of
*Number***
Number Sense

EMC 3025 • © Evan-Moor Corp.

**Understands
the Concept of
*Number***
Number Sense

EMC 3025 • © Evan-Moor Corp.

**Understands
the Concept of
*Number***
Number Sense

EMC 3025 • © Evan-Moor Corp.

**Understands
the Concept of
*Number***
Number Sense

EMC 3025 • © Evan-Moor Corp.

**Understands
the Concept of
*Number***
Number Sense

EMC 3025 • © Evan-Moor Corp.

Understands the Concept of *Number*

| Class Checklist | | Key: | + correct response | – incorrect response | ● self-corrected |

Name	Date	Row 1	2	3	4	Notes
		1	4	3	5	

Note: Student matches a set of objects to a number.

Name _____

Baby Bugs

Match each ladybug to her baby or babies. Draw a line.

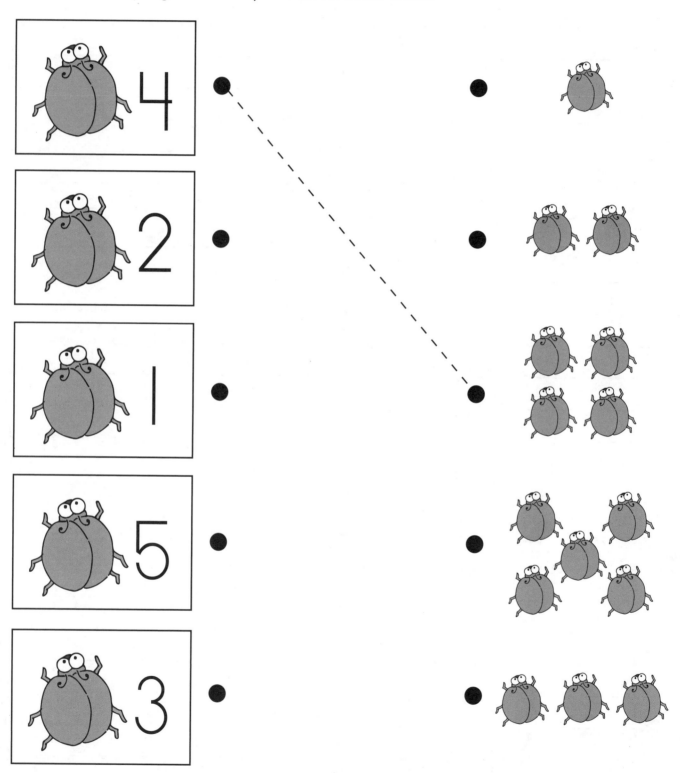

EMC 3025 • Math Assessment Tasks • © Evan-Moor Corp.

Objective:
Student compares two sets of pictured objects and determines which set contains more.

Materials:
Picture Cards, p. 41

Class Checklist, p. 43

Activity Sheet, p. 44

Student Task

Hold the picture cards. Say:

> Today you will look at pictures. You will say which picture shows more. Let's begin.

Place the two heart picture cards on the table. Say:

> Hand me the card that has more hearts.

Student responds. Record the response on the class checklist. Remove the heart cards.

Repeat the procedure modeled above with the two remaining sets of cards.

Number Sense
Knows the Concept of *More Than*   **41**

Knows the Concept of *More Than*

Number Sense

EMC 3025 • © Evan-Moor Corp.

Knows the Concept of *More Than*

Number Sense

EMC 3025 • © Evan-Moor Corp.

Knows the Concept of *More Than*

Number Sense

EMC 3025 • © Evan-Moor Corp.

Knows the Concept of *More Than*

Number Sense

EMC 3025 • © Evan-Moor Corp.

Knows the Concept of *More Than*

Number Sense

EMC 3025 • © Evan-Moor Corp.

Knows the Concept of *More Than*

Number Sense

EMC 3025 • © Evan-Moor Corp.

Knows the Concept of *More Than*

Class Checklist		Key:	**+** correct response	**−** incorrect response	**●** self-corrected	

Name	Date	6 Hearts	8 Stars	5 Circles	Notes

Name _____

Find More

Circle the set that has more.

❶

❷

❸

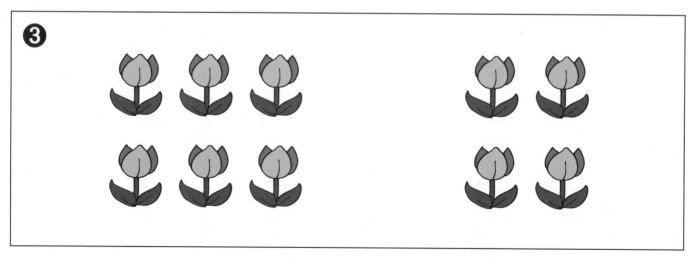

Objective:
Student compares two sets of pictured objects and determines which set has less.

Materials:
Picture Cards, p. 47
Class Checklist, p. 49
Activity Sheet, p. 50

Student Task

Say:

> Today you will look at pictures. You will say which picture shows less. Let's begin.

Place the two picture cards numbered 1 on the table. Say:

> Hand me the card that has less.

Student responds. Record the response on the class checklist. Remove the cards.

Repeat the procedure and the script modeled above with the picture cards numbered 2 and 3.

EMC 3025 • Math Assessment Tasks • © Evan-Moor Corp.

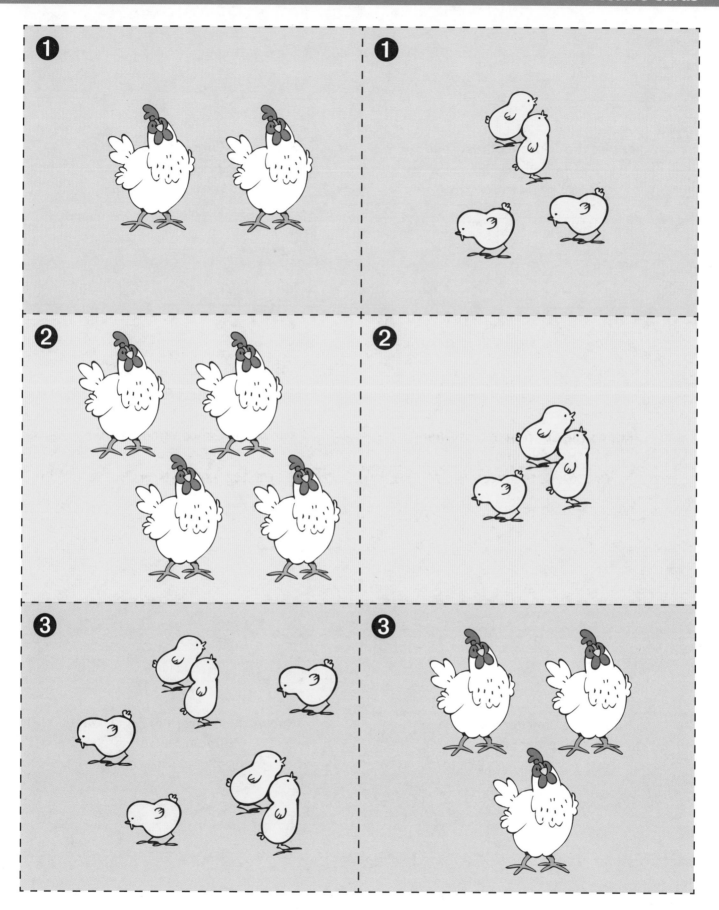

Number Sense
Knows the Concept of *Less Than*   **47**

Knows the Concept of *Less Than*
Number Sense

EMC 3025 • © Evan-Moor Corp.

Knows the Concept of *Less Than*
Number Sense

EMC 3025 • © Evan-Moor Corp.

Knows the Concept of *Less Than*
Number Sense

EMC 3025 • © Evan-Moor Corp.

Knows the Concept of *Less Than*
Number Sense

EMC 3025 • © Evan-Moor Corp.

Knows the Concept of *Less Than*
Number Sense

EMC 3025 • © Evan-Moor Corp.

Knows the Concept of *Less Than*
Number Sense

EMC 3025 • © Evan-Moor Corp.

Knows the Concept of *Less Than*

Class Checklist		Key: + correct response − incorrect response • self-corrected			
Name	Date	Cards 1 2 Chickens	2 3 Chicks	3 3 Chickens	Notes

Name _____

Fun at the Farm

Circle the set that has less.

Number Sense
Knows the Concept of *Less Than*

EMC 3025 • Math Assessment Tasks • © Evan-Moor Corp.

Objective:
Student determines which pictured objects in a row are equal sets.

Materials:
Mat, p. 53

Class Checklist, p. 55

Activity Sheet, p. 56

Blank sheet of paper

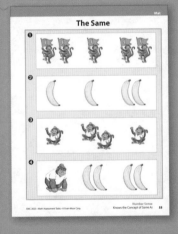

Student Task

Say:

> Today you will point to sets that are the same.

Place the mat in front of the student. Cover all the rows with a blank sheet of paper except row 1. Say:

> Let's begin. Point to the two sets that are the same.

Student responds. Record the response on the class checklist. Move the paper down the mat to reveal row 2. Say:

> Point to the two sets that are the same.

Record the response.

Repeat the procedure and the script modeled above with the two remaining rows.

The Same

1

2

3

4

Knows the Concept of *Same As*
Number Sense

EMC 3025 • © Evan-Moor Corp.

Knows the Concept of *Same As*

Quick Checks

Class Checklist		Key: + correct response − incorrect response • self-corrected				
Name	Date	Row 1 Sets of 2 Monkeys	2 Sets of 1 Banana	3 Sets of 1 Monkey	4 Sets of 2 Bananas	Notes

Note: Student determines which sets have the same amount.

Name _____

Same Sets

Circle the sets that are the same in each row.

❶

❷

❸

❹

Objective:
Student orders the numbers 1 to 6 from smallest to largest.

Materials:
Number Cards, p. 59

Class Checklist, p. 61

Activity Sheet, p. 62

Student Task

Say:

> Today you will make a dog using number cards.

Place the number cards faceup on the table in random order. Place number card 1, the dog's head, in front of the student. Say:

> Let's begin. Put the number that comes after 1 on the table. Say the number.

Student responds. Say:

> Now put the number that comes next on the table. Say the number.

Student responds.

Repeat the procedure and the script modeled above with the remaining number cards. Use the completed dog as a reference for recording the student's responses on the class checklist.

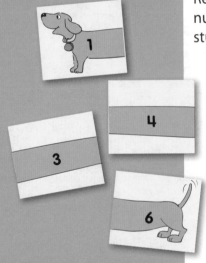

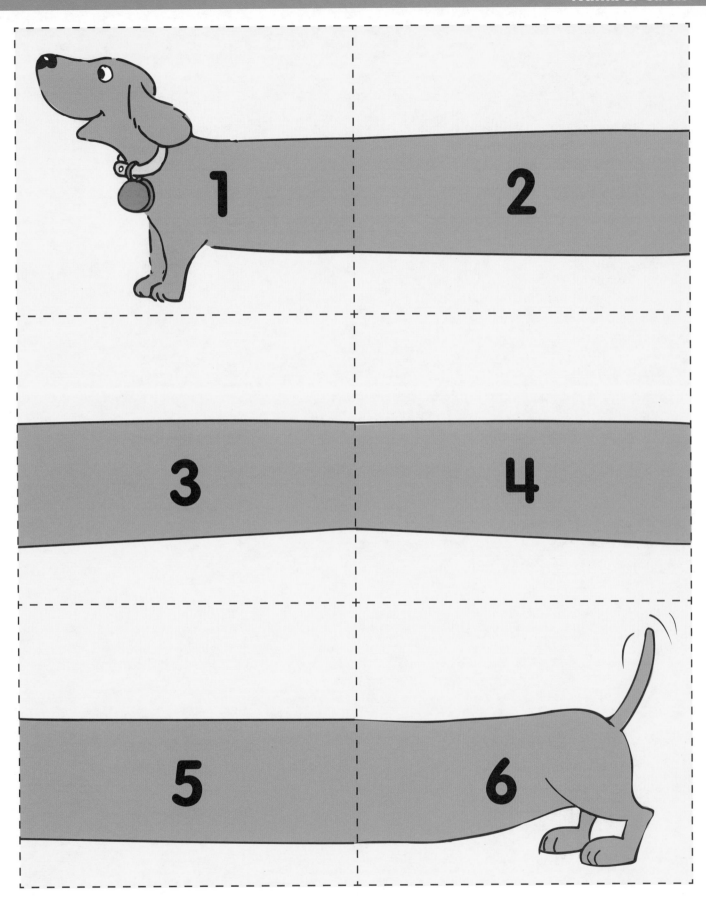

Orders Numbers

Number Sense

EMC 3025 • © Evan-Moor Corp.

Orders Numbers

Number Sense

EMC 3025 • © Evan-Moor Corp.

Orders Numbers

Number Sense

EMC 3025 • © Evan-Moor Corp.

Orders Numbers

Number Sense

EMC 3025 • © Evan-Moor Corp.

Orders Numbers

Number Sense

EMC 3025 • © Evan-Moor Corp.

Orders Numbers

Number Sense

EMC 3025 • © Evan-Moor Corp.

Orders Numbers

Class Checklist		Key: + all numbers correct • self-corrected number List each incorrectly ordered number.
Name	Date	Notes

Name _____

Hand in Hand

Cut. Glue in order. Use a long sheet of paper.

Objective:
Student indentifies the position of objects in a sequence.

Materials:
Animal Cards, pp. 65 and 67

Class Checklist, p. 69

Activity Sheet, p. 70

Student Task

Say:

> Today you will answer my questions about some animal cards.

Place the animal cards in order on the table, forming a long line. Use the numbers on the back of the cards as reference. Say:

> Let's begin. What animal is first in line?

Student responds. Record the response on the class checklist.

Ask the following questions in order, stopping after each response to record. Say:

> What animal is third in line?
> What animal is last in line?
> In what place is the rabbit?
> In what place is the raccoon?

Number Sense
Understands Ordinal Numbers

2

Understands Ordinal Numbers
Number Sense

EMC 3025 • © Evan-Moor Corp.

1

Understands Ordinal Numbers
Number Sense

EMC 3025 • © Evan-Moor Corp.

4

Understands Ordinal Numbers
Number Sense

EMC 3025 • © Evan-Moor Corp.

3

Understands Ordinal Numbers
Number Sense

EMC 3025 • © Evan-Moor Corp.

6

Understands Ordinal Numbers
Number Sense

EMC 3025 • © Evan-Moor Corp.

5

Understands Ordinal Numbers
Number Sense

EMC 3025 • © Evan-Moor Corp.

8

Understands Ordinal Numbers
Number Sense

EMC 3025 • © Evan-Moor Corp.

7

Understands Ordinal Numbers
Number Sense

EMC 3025 • © Evan-Moor Corp.

Understands Ordinal Numbers

Class Checklist		Key: + correct response − incorrect response ● self-corrected					
Name	Date	Dog is first.	Cat is third.	Bear is last.	Rabbit is fifth.	Raccoon is fourth.	Notes

Name _____

In Line

Cut. Glue the first. Glue the second.

Glue the third. Glue the fourth.

Adds Concrete Objects

Objective:
Student uses manipulatives to take one away.

Materials:
Mat, p. 73
Dog Bone Cards, p. 75
Class Checklist, p. 77
Activity Sheet, p. 78

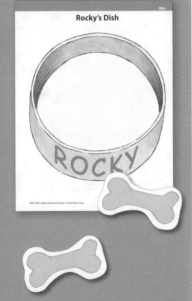

Student Task

Say:

> Today you will tell me how much *one more* is.

Place the dog bone cards faceup on the table. Place the mat in front of the student. Put one dog bone card in the dish. Say:

> Let's begin. There's 1 bone in the dog dish. Add 1 more bone.

After the student places the bone in the dish, say:

> How many dog bones?

Student responds. Record the response on the class checklist. Say:

> Now there are 2 dog bones. Add 1 more dog bone.

After the student places the bone in the dish, say:

> How many dog bones?

Record the response. Say:

> Now there are 3 dog bones. Add 1 more dog bone.

After the student places the bone in the dish, say:

> How many dog bones?

Record the response.

Rocky's Dish

Number Sense
Adds Concrete Objects **73**

Adds Concrete Objects
Number Sense

EMC 3025 • © Evan-Moor Corp.

EMC 3025 • Math Assessment Tasks • © Evan-Moor Corp.

Bones

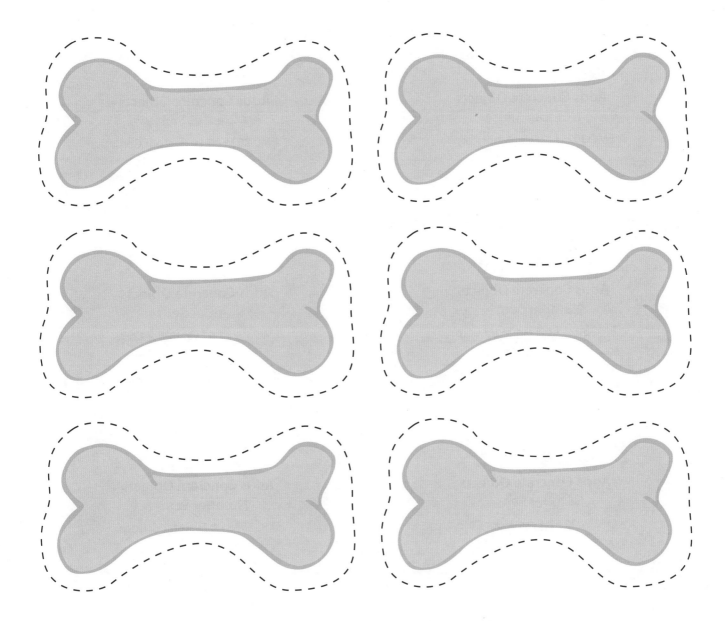

Number Sense
Adds Concrete Objects **75**

Adds Concrete Objects
Number Sense

EMC 3025 • © Evan-Moor Corp.

Adds Concrete Objects
Number Sense

EMC 3025 • © Evan-Moor Corp.

Adds Concrete Objects
Number Sense

EMC 3025 • © Evan-Moor Corp.

Adds Concrete Objects
Number Sense

EMC 3025 • © Evan-Moor Corp.

Adds Concrete Objects
Number Sense

EMC 3025 • © Evan-Moor Corp.

Adds Concrete Objects
Number Sense

EMC 3025 • © Evan-Moor Corp.

Adds Concrete Objects

Class Checklist		Key: + correct response	− incorrect response	• self-corrected	
Name	Date	1 + 1 = 2	2 + 1 = 3	3 + 1 = 4	Notes

Name _____

One More

1 Draw 1 more bone.

Circle how many bones.　　1　　2　　3

2 Draw one more ball.

Circle how many balls.　　3　　4　　5

3 Draw 1 more house.

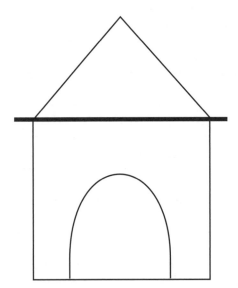

Circle how many houses.　　2　　3　　4

Objective:
Student uses manipulatives to take one away.

Materials:
Flower Cards, p. 81
Class Checklist, p. 83
Activity Sheet, p. 84

Student Task

Say:

> Today you will tell me how much *one less* is.
> Let's begin.

Place four flower cards on the table. Count aloud as you place each flower. Say:

> Here are 4 flowers. Take 1 away.

Student removes one flower. Say:

> How many flowers are left?

Student counts and responds. Record the response on the class checklist.

Remove the flowers. Place five flowers on the table and count aloud as you place each one. Then say:

> Here are 5 flowers. Take 1 away.

Student removes one flower. Say:

> How many flowers are left?

Record the response. Remove the flowers. Place three flowers on the table and count aloud as you place each one. Say:

> Here are 3 flowers. Take 1 away.

Student removes one flower. Say:

> How many flowers are left?

Record the response.

EMC 3025 • Math Assessment Tasks • © Evan-Moor Corp.

Subtracts Concrete Objects

Number Sense

EMC 3025 • © Evan-Moor Corp.

Subtracts Concrete Objects

Number Sense

EMC 3025 • © Evan-Moor Corp.

Subtracts Concrete Objects

Number Sense

EMC 3025 • © Evan-Moor Corp.

Subtracts Concrete Objects

Number Sense

EMC 3025 • © Evan-Moor Corp.

Subtracts Concrete Objects

Number Sense

EMC 3025 • © Evan-Moor Corp.

Subtracts Concrete Objects

Number Sense

EMC 3025 • © Evan-Moor Corp.

Subtracts Concrete Objects

Class Checklist		Key:	**+** correct response	**−** incorrect response	● self-corrected	

Name	Date	4 – 1 = 3	5 – 1 = 4	3 – 1 = 2	Notes

Note: Student subtracts concrete objects.

Name _____

Pick the Flowers

How many are left?
Circle the number.

❶

2   3   4

❷

1   2   3

❸

3   4   5

❹

1   2   3

Checks

Unit 2
Measurement and Geometry

Recognizes Shapes

Quick
Checks

Objective:
Student discerns four simple plane shapes in a drawing.

Materials:
Mat, p. 89

Class Checklist, p. 91

Activity Sheet, p. 92

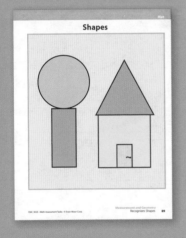

Student Task

Say:

> Today you will find shapes in a picture.

Place the mat in front of the student. Say:

> Let's begin. Look at the picture. Point to the circle.

Student responds. Record the response on the class checklist. Then say:

> Point to the triangle.

Record the response. Then say:

> Point to the square.

Record the response. Then say:

> Point to the rectangle on the house.

Record the response. Then say:

> Point to the rectangle on the tree.

Record the response.

Measurement and Geometry
Recognizes Shapes

Shapes

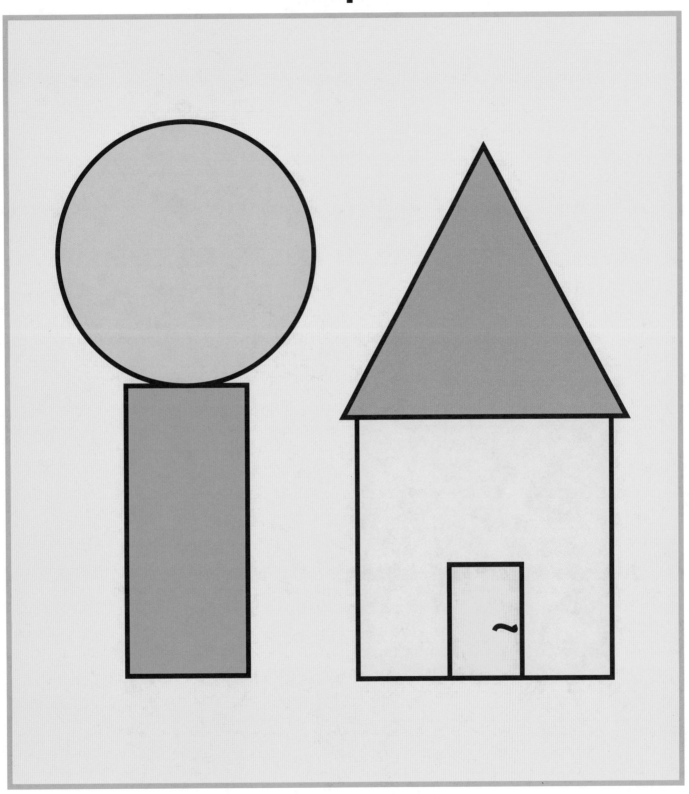

Recognizes Shapes

Measurement and Geometry

EMC 3025 • © Evan-Moor Corp.

Recognizes Shapes

Class Checklist		Key: + correct response − incorrect response • self-corrected					
Name	Date	Circle	Triangle	Square	Rectangle on House	Rectangle on Tree	Notes

Name _____

Color the Shapes

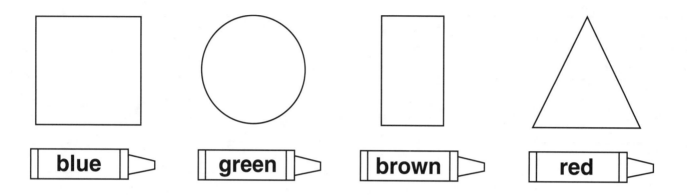

blue   green   brown   red

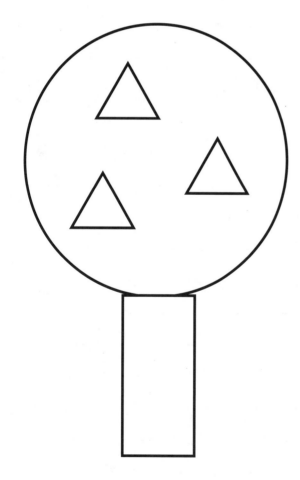

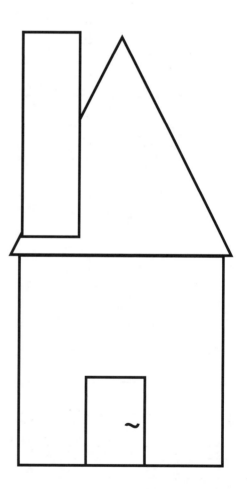

Matches Shapes

Objective:
Student matches plane shapes of different sizes and colors.

Materials:
Mat, p. 95

Shape Cards, p. 97

Class Checklist, p. 99

Activity Sheet, p. 100

Blank sheet of paper

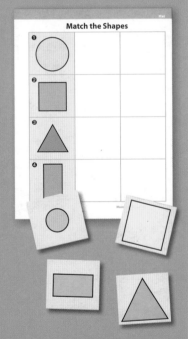

Model the Task

Say:

> Today you are going to match shapes. I will show you what to do.

Arrange the shape cards faceup in rows. Place them in random order. Place the mat in front of the student. Use a blank sheet of paper to cover all the rows except row 1. Point to the circle in row 1 and say:

> Let's begin. Here is a circle. I will put a circle shape that matches it on the mat.

Place one of the circle shape cards in row 1.

Student Task

Say:

> Now it's your turn. Put a circle shape on the mat.

Student responds. Record the response on the class checklist. Move the paper down the mat to reveal row 2. Say:

> Look at this square. Put two square shapes that match on the mat.

Record the response. Repeat the procedure with the triangle in row 3 and the rectangle in row 4.

Match the Shapes

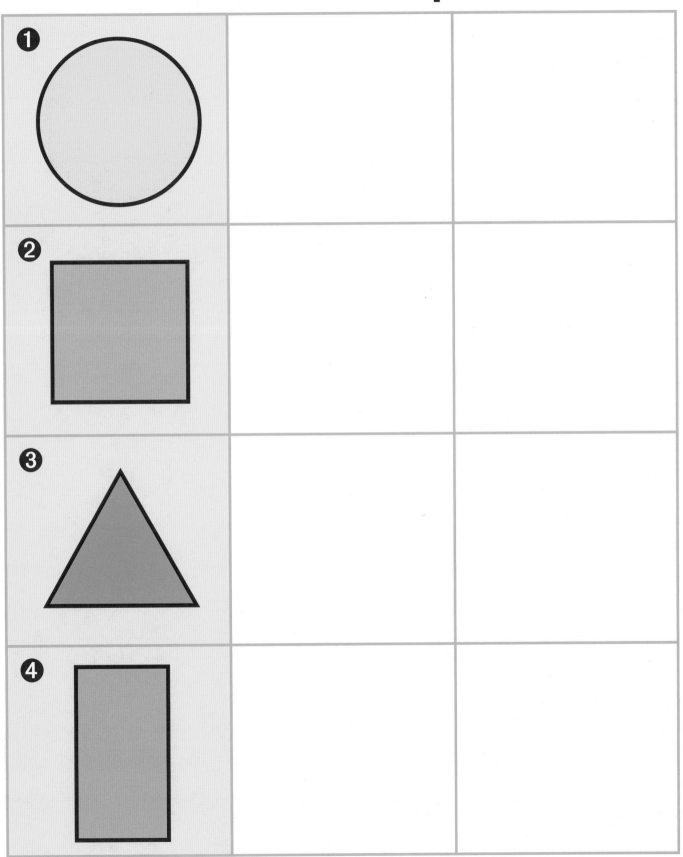

Matches Shapes

Measurement and Geometry

EMC 3025 • © Evan-Moor Corp.

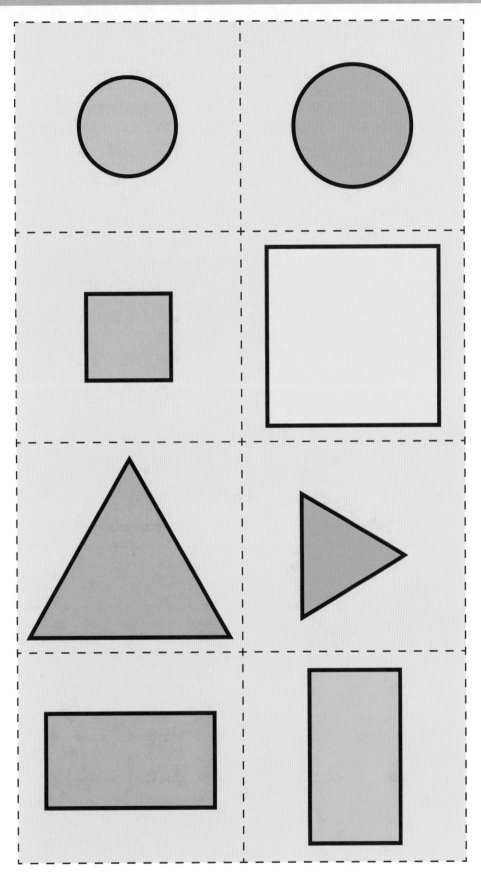

Measurement and Geometry
Matches Shapes **97**

Matches Shapes

Measurement and Geometry

EMC 3025 • © Evan-Moor Corp.

Matches Shapes

Measurement and Geometry

EMC 3025 • © Evan-Moor Corp.

Matches Shapes

Measurement and Geometry

EMC 3025 • © Evan-Moor Corp.

Matches Shapes

Measurement and Geometry

EMC 3025 • © Evan-Moor Corp.

Matches Shapes

Measurement and Geometry

EMC 3025 • © Evan-Moor Corp.

Matches Shapes

Measurement and Geometry

EMC 3025 • © Evan-Moor Corp.

Matches Shapes

Measurement and Geometry

EMC 3025 • © Evan-Moor Corp.

Matches Shapes

Measurement and Geometry

EMC 3025 • © Evan-Moor Corp.

Matches Shapes

Class Checklist		Key: **+** correct response **−** incorrect response **●** self-corrected				
Name	Date	Matches Circle	Matches Squares	Matches Triangles	Matches Rectangles	Notes

EMC 3025 • Math Assessment Tasks • © Evan-Moor Corp.

Name _____

Match Up

Match the shapes.
Draw a line.

Follows Directions About Location

Objective:

Student displays a knowledge of direction and position by arranging objects as directed.

Materials:

Mat, p. 103

Picture Cards, p. 105

Class Checklist, p. 107

Activity Sheet, p. 108

Student Task

Say:

> Today you will follow my directions. You will use a cat, a dog, a doghouse, and a ball.

Place the picture cards faceup on the table. Place the mat in front of the student. Say:

> Let's begin. Put the doghouse **next to** the tree.

Student responds. Record the response on the class checklist.

Give the directions that follow. Stop after each student response to record. Say:

> Put the ball **under** the tree.
>
> Put the dog **on top of** the doghouse.
>
> Put the dog **in front of** the doghouse.
>
> Make the cat go **up** the tree.
>
> Make the cat go **down** the tree.
>
> Put the dog **inside** the doghouse.
>
> Put the dog **outside** the doghouse.

Where's Rocky?

Measurement and Geometry
Follows Directions About Location   **103**

Follows Directions About Location

Measurement and Geometry

EMC 3025 • © Evan-Moor Corp.

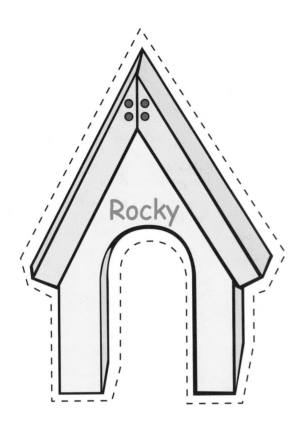

Rocky

**Follows Directions
About Location**
Measurement and
Geometry
EMC 3025
© Evan-Moor Corp.

**Follows Directions
About Location**
Measurement and Geometry
EMC 3025 • © Evan-Moor Corp.

**Follows Directions
About Location**
Measurement and
Geometry
EMC 3025
© Evan-Moor Corp.

**Follows Directions
About Location**
Measurement and
Geometry
EMC 3025
© Evan-Moor Corp.

Follows Directions About Location

Name	Date	Next To	Under	On Top Of	In Front Of	Up	Down	Inside	Outside	Notes

Class Checklist

Key: + correct response — incorrect response ● self-corrected

Name _____

At the Barn

Put the owl **on top of** the barn. Put the mouse **under** the hay.
Put the pig **next to** the barn. Put the sheep **in front of** the barn.

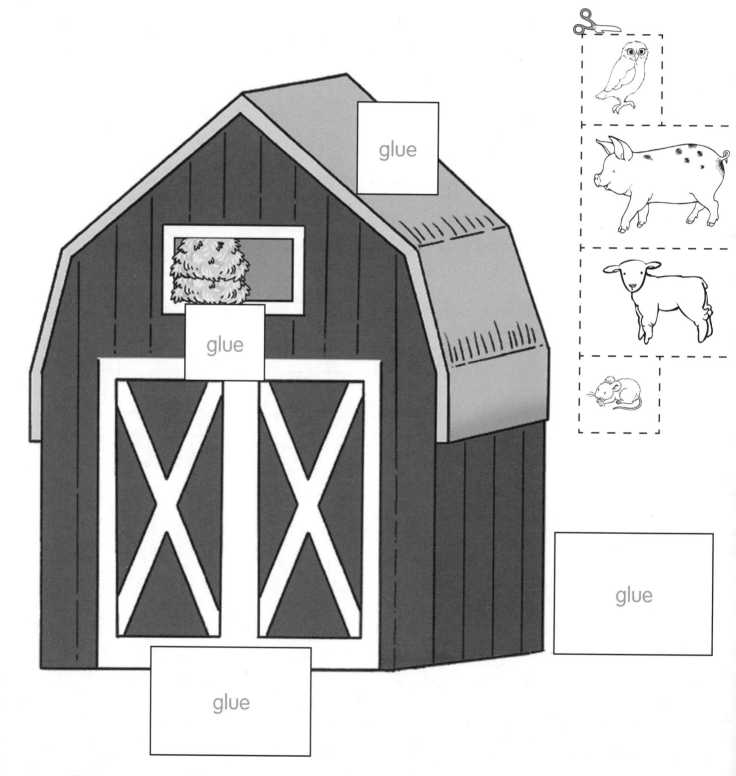

Objective:

Student makes a direct comparison of the length of pictured objects.

Materials:

Material Cards, p. 111

Class Checklist, p. 113

Activity Sheet, p. 114

Student Task

(Note: You will show pairs of cards to the student. When presenting each pair, arrange one card directly under the other.)

Say:

> Today you will show me what is **long** and what is **short.**

Arrange the first set of picture cards on the table. Say:

> Let's begin. Point to the shoe that is **longer.**

Student responds. Record the response on the class checklist. Arrange the second set of picture cards on the table. Say:

> Point to the crayon that is **shorter.**

Record the response. Arrange the third set of picture cards. Say:

> Point to the hair that is **longer.**

Record the response. Arrange the fourth set of picture cards. Say:

> Point to the train that is **shorter.**

Record the response.

Measurement and Geometry
Knows the Concept of *Longer, Shorter*   **111**

Knows the Concept of *Longer, Shorter*
Measurement and Geometry
EMC 3025 • © Evan-Moor Corp.

Knows the Concept of *Longer, Shorter*
Measurement and Geometry
EMC 3025 • © Evan-Moor Corp.

Knows the Concept of *Longer, Shorter*
Measurement and Geometry
EMC 3025 • © Evan-Moor Corp.

Knows the Concept of *Longer, Shorter*
Measurement and Geometry
EMC 3025 • © Evan-Moor Corp.

Knows the Concept of *Longer, Shorter*
Measurement and Geometry
EMC 3025 • © Evan-Moor Corp.

Knows the Concept of *Longer, Shorter*
Measurement and Geometry
EMC 3025 • © Evan-Moor Corp.

Knows the Concept of *Longer, Shorter*
Measurement and Geometry
EMC 3025 • © Evan-Moor Corp.

Knows the Concept of *Longer, Shorter*
Measurement and Geometry
EMC 3025 • © Evan-Moor Corp.

Knows the Concept of *Longer, Shorter*

Class Checklist		Key: + correct response − incorrect response • self-corrected				
Name	Date	Yellow shoe is longer.	Red crayon is shorter.	Brown hair is longer.	Train with 1 car is shorter.	Notes

Name _____

Longer or Shorter?

Circle.

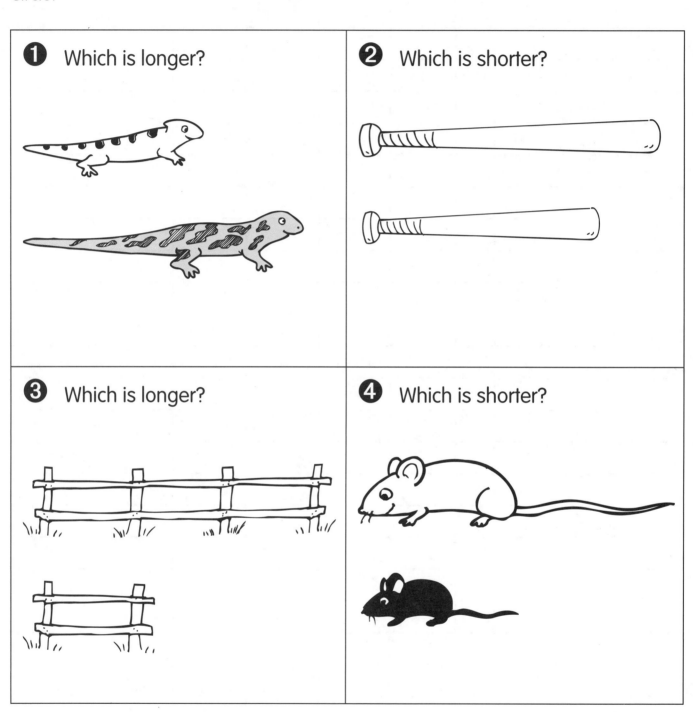

1 Which is longer?

2 Which is shorter?

3 Which is longer?

4 Which is shorter?

Recognizes and Sequences a Day's Events

Objective:

Student recognizes basic time concepts and sequences personal events that occur in the morning, in the afternoon, and at night.

Materials:

Mat, p. 117

Picture Cards, p. 119

Class Checklist, p. 121

Activity Sheet, p. 122

Student Task

Say:

> Today you will show what you do during the day.

Place the mat in front of the student. Place the picture cards on the table faceup in random order. (If you wish, read the cards to the student.) Say:

> Let's begin. Find two pictures that show what you do in the morning.

Student takes the two cards. Point to the image and word in row 1 on the mat and say:

> This says **morning.** Pick the card that shows what you do **first** in the morning. Put the card on the mat.

Student places the card. Then ask the student to place the other card.

Point to the image and word in row 2 and say:

> This says **afternoon.** Find two pictures that show what you can do in the afternoon. *(Pause while student responds.)* Now put the card on the mat that shows what you do **first.** *(Pause while student responds.)* Now put the other card on the mat.

Point to the image and word in row 3 and say:

> This says **night.** Put the card that shows what you do **first** at night. *(Pause while student responds.)* Now put the other card on the mat.

Use the completed mat as a reference for recording the student's responses on the class checklist.

A Busy Day

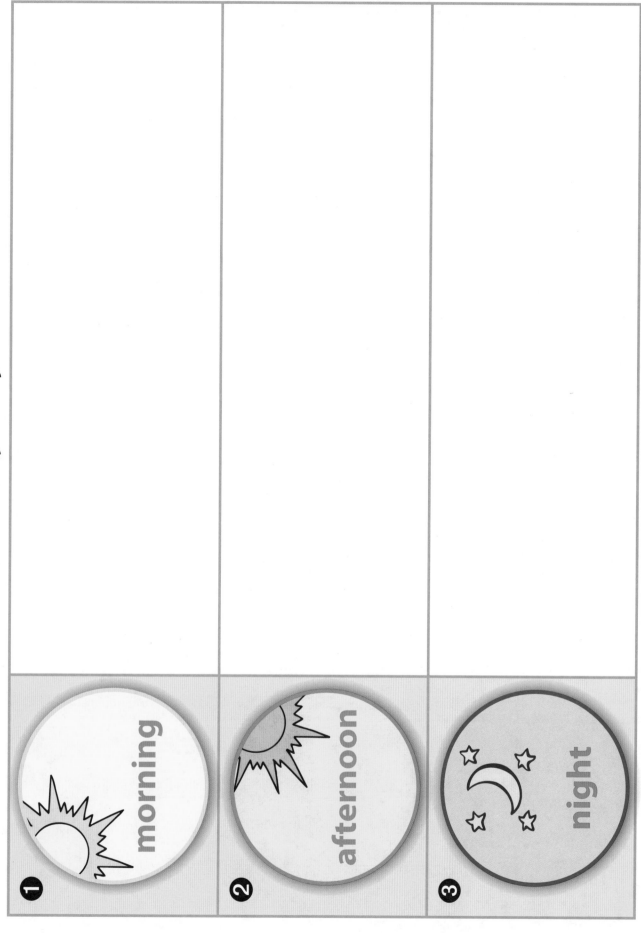

1 morning

2 afternoon

3 night

Measurement and Geometry
Recognizes and Sequences a Day's Events **117**

Recognizes and Sequences a Day's Events

Measurement and Geometry

EMC 3025 • © Evan-Moor Corp.

wake up

eat breakfast

wash hands

eat

brush teeth

fall asleep

Measurement and Geometry
Recognizes and Sequences a Day's Events   **119**

Recognizes and Sequences a Day's Events
Measurement and Geometry

EMC 3025 • © Evan-Moor Corp.

Recognizes and Sequences a Day's Events
Measurement and Geometry

EMC 3025 • © Evan-Moor Corp.

Recognizes and Sequences a Day's Events
Measurement and Geometry

EMC 3025 • © Evan-Moor Corp.

Recognizes and Sequences a Day's Events
Measurement and Geometry

EMC 3025 • © Evan-Moor Corp.

Recognizes and Sequences a Day's Events
Measurement and Geometry

EMC 3025 • © Evan-Moor Corp.

Recognizes and Sequences a Day's Events
Measurement and Geometry

EMC 3025 • © Evan-Moor Corp.

Recognizes and Sequences a Day's Events

Class Checklist		Key:	**+** correct response	**–** incorrect response	● self-corrected	
Name	Date	Morning	Afternoon	Night	Notes	

Note: Student recognizes a day's events.

Name _____

My Day

Draw something you do at each time of day.

morning

afternoon

night

Objective:

Student uses non-standard units of measurement to measure the length and height of pictured objects.

Materials:

Mat, p. 125

Picture Cards, p. 127

Class Checklist, p. 129

Activity Sheet, p. 130

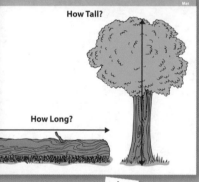

Student Task

Say:

> Today you will measure some pictures.

Place the snail and the dragonfly picture cards in two separate piles on the table. Place the mat in front of the student. Call attention to the log. Say:

> Let's begin. Put snails on the log. Find out how many snails **long** the log is.

Student places snails on the log and says how many snails long the log is. Record the response on the class checklist.

Call attention to the tree on the mat. Say:

> Put dragonflies on the tree. Find out how many dragonflies **tall** the tree is.

Student places the dragonflies on the tree and says how many dragonflies tall the tree is. Record the response.

EMC 3025 • Math Assessment Tasks • © Evan-Moor Corp.

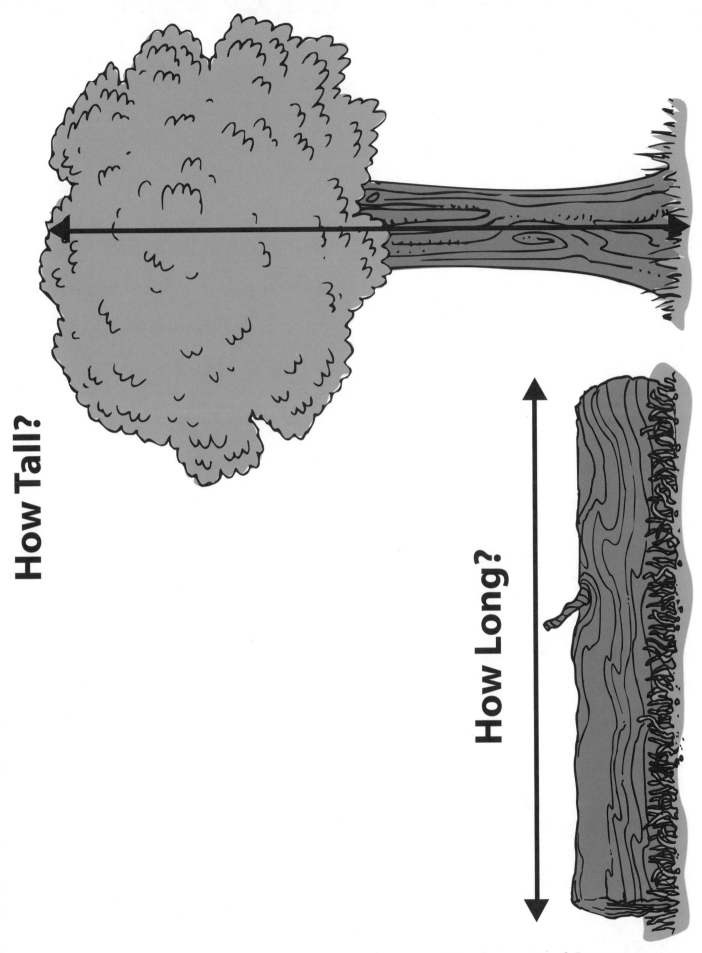

How Tall?

How Long?

Measurement and Geometry
Uses Nonstandard Units of Measurement **125**

Uses Nonstandard Units of Measurement

Measurement and Geometry

EMC 3025 • © Evan-Moor Corp.

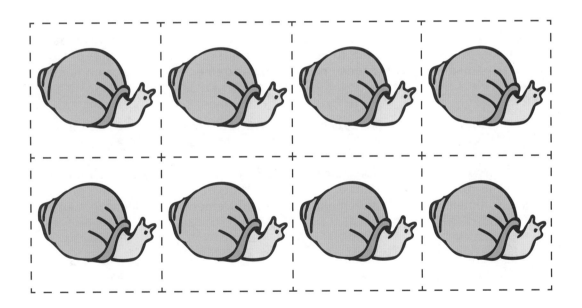

Measurement and Geometry
Uses Nonstandard Units of Measurement   **127**

**Uses Nonstandard
Units of
Measurement**
Measurement and
Geometry

EMC 3025
© Evan-Moor Corp.

**Uses Nonstandard
Units of
Measurement**
Measurement and
Geometry

EMC 3025
© Evan-Moor Corp.

**Uses Nonstandard
Units of
Measurement**
Measurement and
Geometry

EMC 3025
© Evan-Moor Corp.

**Uses Nonstandard
Units of
Measurement**
Measurement and
Geometry

EMC 3025
© Evan-Moor Corp.

**Uses Nonstandard
Units of
Measurement**
Measurement and
Geometry

EMC 3025
© Evan-Moor Corp.

**Uses Nonstandard
Units of
Measurement**
Measurement and
Geometry

EMC 3025
© Evan-Moor Corp.

**Uses Nonstandard
Units of
Measurement**
Measurement and
Geometry

EMC 3025
© Evan-Moor Corp.

**Uses Nonstandard
Units of
Measurement**
Measurement and
Geometry

EMC 3025
© Evan-Moor Corp.

**Uses Nonstandard
Units of
Measurement**
Measurement and
Geometry

EMC 3025
© Evan-Moor Corp.

**Uses Nonstandard
Units of
Measurement**
Measurement and
Geometry

EMC 3025
© Evan-Moor Corp.

**Uses Nonstandard
Units of
Measurement**
Measurement and
Geometry

EMC 3025
© Evan-Moor Corp.

**Uses Nonstandard
Units of
Measurement**
Measurement and
Geometry

EMC 3025
© Evan-Moor Corp.

**Uses Nonstandard
Units of
Measurement**
Measurement and
Geometry

EMC 3025
© Evan-Moor Corp.

**Uses Nonstandard
Units of
Measurement**
Measurement and
Geometry

EMC 3025
© Evan-Moor Corp.

**Uses Nonstandard
Units of
Measurement**
Measurement and
Geometry

EMC 3025
© Evan-Moor Corp.

**Uses Nonstandard
Units of
Measurement**
Measurement and
Geometry

EMC 3025
© Evan-Moor Corp.

Uses Nonstandard Units of Measurement

Class Checklist		Key: **+** correct response **−** incorrect response **•** self-corrected		
Name	Date	The log is 4 snails long.	The tree is 5 dragonflies tall.	Notes

EMC 3025 • Math Assessment Tasks • © Evan-Moor Corp.

Name _____

How Long Is the Pond?

Cut out and glue the ducks.
Write the answer.

The pond is _____ ducks long.

The pond is _____ ducks long.

Unit 3
Statistics, Data Analysis, and Probability

Unit 4
Algebra and Functions

Objective:

Student names three different patterns.

Materials:

Mat, p. 135

Class Checklist, p. 137

Activity Sheet, p. 138

Blank sheet of paper

Student Task

Say:

> Today you will tell me the patterns you see.

Place the mat on the table. Cover all the rows with a blank sheet of paper except for row 1. Say:

> Let's begin. Look at the pictures in row 1. Tell me the pattern.

Record the student's response. You may find that individual students name the patterns differently. Reasonable responses, such as Girl Boy, Girl Boy, Girl Boy, or AB AB AB, are correct.

Move the paper down the mat to reveal row 2. Say:

> Look at the pictures in row 2. Tell me the pattern.

Record the student's response. Reasonable responses, such as Cat Cat Dog, Cat Cat Dog, or AAB AAB, are correct.

Move the paper down the mat to reveal row 3. Say:

> Look at the pictures in row 3. Tell me the pattern.

Record the student's response. Reasonable responses, such as Girl on Skates, Girl on Bike, Girl on Bike, Girl on Skates, Girl on Bike, Girl on Bike, or ABB ABB, are correct.

Patterns

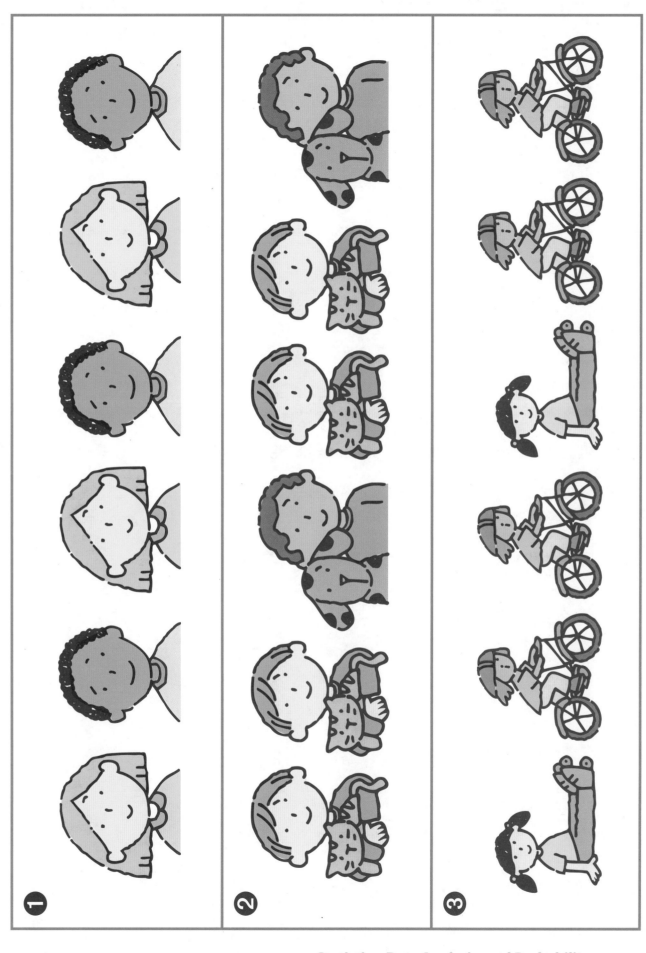

① ② ③

Statistics, Data Analysis, and Probability
Recognizes Patterns **135**

Recognizes Patterns

Statistics, Data Analysis, and Probability

EMC 3025 • © Evan-Moor Corp.

Recognizes Patterns

Class Checklist		Key: + correct response − incorrect response ● self-corrected			
Name	Date	Row 1	Row 2	Row 3	Notes

Statistics, Data Analysis, and Probability

Name _____

Activity Sheet

Suns and Moons

Cut.
Glue what is missing.

Statistics, Data Analysis, and Probability
Recognizes Patterns

EMC 3025 • Math Assessment Tasks • © Evan-Moor Corp.

Extends Patterns

Objective:

Student extends three given patterns.

Materials:

Mat, p. 141

Picture Cards, p. 141

Class Checklist, p. 143

Activity Sheet, p. 144

Blank sheet of paper

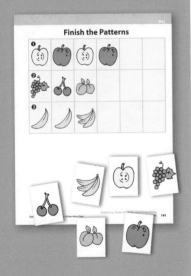

Student Task

Say:

> Today you will finish patterns of fruit.

Spread the picture cards on the table faceup and in rows. Place the mat in front of the student. Cover all of the rows on the mat except row 1. Say:

> Let's begin with row 1. Put the pictures on the mat that finish the pattern.

(Note: Student may say the names of the pictures before adding cards.) Student places cards on the mat. Record the response on the class checklist. Then move the paper down the mat to reveal row 2. Say:

> Put the pictures on the mat that finish the pattern in row 2.

Record the response. Move the paper down the mat to reveal row 3. Say:

> Put the pictures on the mat that finish the pattern in row 3.

Record the response.

Finish the Patterns

Statistics, Data Analysis, and Probability
Extends Patterns **141**

Extends Patterns

Statistics, Data Analysis, and Probability

EMC 3025 • © Evan-Moor Corp.

Extends Patterns

Statistics, Data Analysis, and Probability

EMC 3025
© Evan-Moor Corp.

Extends Patterns

Statistics, Data Analysis, and Probability

EMC 3025
© Evan-Moor Corp.

Extends Patterns

Statistics, Data Analysis, and Probability

EMC 3025
© Evan-Moor Corp.

Extends Patterns

Statistics, Data Analysis, and Probability

EMC 3025
© Evan-Moor Corp.

Extends Patterns

Statistics, Data Analysis, and Probability

EMC 3025
© Evan-Moor Corp.

Extends Patterns

Statistics, Data Analysis, and Probability

EMC 3025
© Evan-Moor Corp.

Extends Patterns

Statistics, Data Analysis, and Probability

EMC 3025
© Evan-Moor Corp.

Extends Patterns

Statistics, Data Analysis, and Probability

EMC 3025
© Evan-Moor Corp.

Extends Patterns

Statistics, Data Analysis, and Probability

EMC 3025
© Evan-Moor Corp.

Extends Patterns

Statistics, Data Analysis, and Probability

EMC 3025
© Evan-Moor Corp.

Extends Patterns

Class Checklist		Key:	+ correct response	− incorrect response	● self-corrected	

Name	Date	Row 1	Row 2	Row 3	Notes

Statistics, Data Analysis, and Probability

Note: Student extends patterns.

Name _____

Next!

Draw what comes next.

1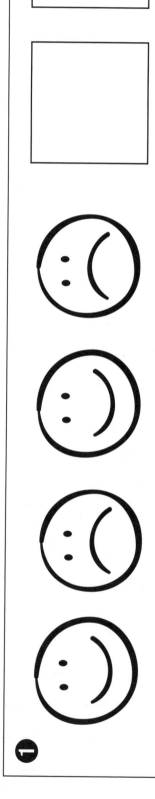

2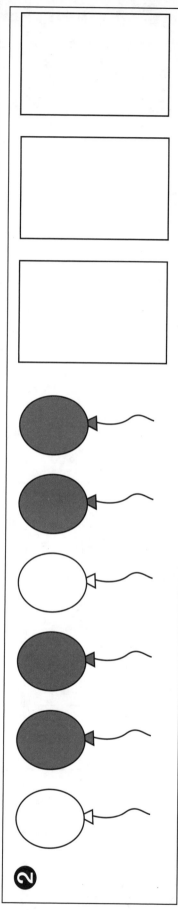

3

Analyzes Data

Objective:

Student answers questions with information gained from a graph.

Materials:

Mat, p. 147

Class Checklist, p. 149

Activity Sheet, p. 150

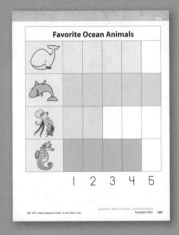

Student Task

Say:

> Today you will read a graph that has pictures.

Place the mat in front of the student. Point to the title of the graph as you say:

> Let's begin. The graph shows some people's favorite ocean animals. What are the animals?

Student tells the names of the four pictured animals. Record the response on the class checklist. Then say:

> Which animal did the most people like?

Record the response. The student may respond to all of your questions by saying the name of the animal or by pointing to its picture. Say:

> Which animal did the fewest people like?

Record the student's response. Say:

> What two animals did the same number of people like?

Record the response. Say:

> How many people liked the octopus the best?

Favorite Ocean Animals

1   2   3   4   5

Analyzes Data

Analyzes Data

Class Checklist		Key: **+** correct response **−** incorrect response **●** self-corrected					
Name	Date	Whale, Shark, Octopus, Sea Horse	Most liked the shark.	Fewest liked the octopus.	Same number liked the whale and sea horse.	2 liked the octopus best.	Notes

Name _____

Activity Sheet

How Many Do You See?

Count.
Color a box for every fish and snail.

1	2	3	4

Which has the most?

EMC 3025 • Math Assessment Tasks • © Evan-Moor Corp.

Objective:
Student sorts pictured figures by shape and by size.

Materials:
Mat, p. 153

Shape Cards, p. 155

Class Checklist, p. 157

Activity Sheet, p. 158

Student Task

Say:

> Today you will sort pictures.

Spread the shape cards faceup on the table in random order. Place the mat in front of the student. Point to areas 1 and 2 on the mat as you say:

> Let's begin. Sort the pictures by shape. Put one kind of shape here. Put the other shape here.

Student places the circles in one area and the squares in the other. Use the completed mat as a reference for recording the response on the class checklist. Use the section labeled **Sorts by Shape**.

Then clear the mat. Spread the cards faceup on the table. Say:

> Now sort the pictures by size. Put the small shapes in one area. Put the big shapes in the other area.

Student sorts the figures into small and big figures. (One area should have two small circles and two small squares. One area has a big circle and a big square.)

Record the response. Use the section on the class checklist labeled **Sorts by Size.**

Sorting

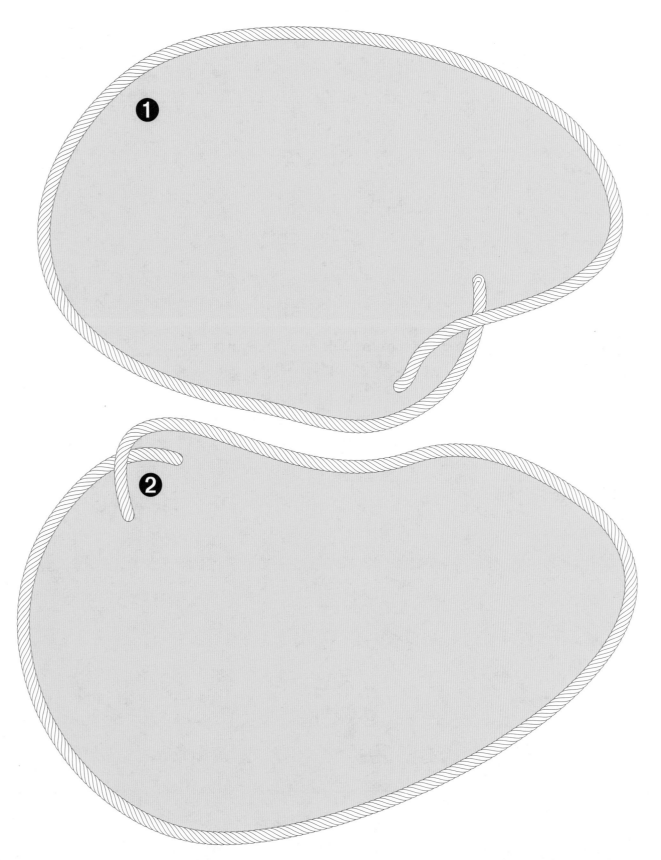

Algebra and Functions
Sorts and Regroups Objects by One Attribute   **153**

Sorts and Regroups Objects by One Attribute
Algebra and Functions

EMC 3025 • © Evan-Moor Corp.

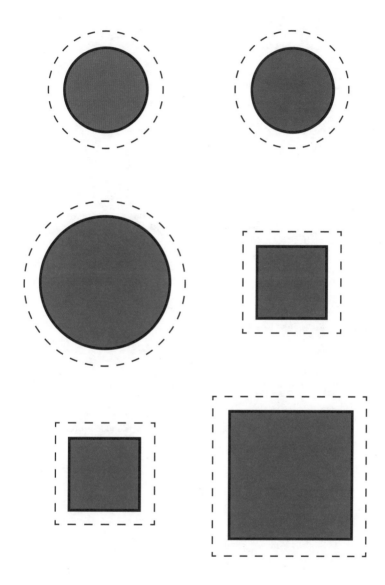

Algebra and Functions
Sorts and Regroups Objects by One Attribute   **155**

**Sorts and Regroups
Objects by One Attribute**

Algebra and Functions

EMC 3025
© Evan-Moor Corp.

**Sorts and Regroups
Objects by One Attribute**

Algebra and Functions

EMC 3025
© Evan-Moor Corp.

**Sorts and Regroups
Objects by One
Attribute**

Algebra and
Functions

EMC 3025
© Evan-Moor Corp.

**Sorts and Regroups
Objects by One Attribute**

Algebra and Functions

EMC 3025
© Evan-Moor Corp.

**Sorts and Regroups
Objects by One Attribute**

Algebra and Functions

EMC 3025
© Evan-Moor Corp.

**Sorts and Regroups
Objects by One
Attribute**

Algebra and
Functions

EMC 3025
© Evan-Moor Corp.

Sorts and Regroups Objects by One Attribute

Class Checklist		Key: **+** correct response	**–** incorrect response	● self-corrected

Name	Date	Sorts by Shape	Sorts by Size	Notes

Algebra and Functions
Sorts and Regroups Objects by One Attribute

Name _____

Sort the Cookies

Cut out the cookies.
Sort by shape.
Glue.

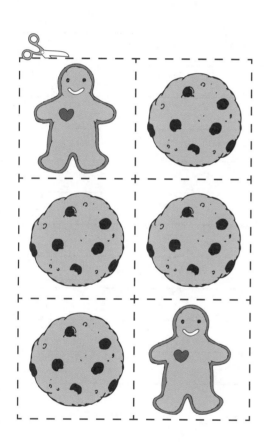

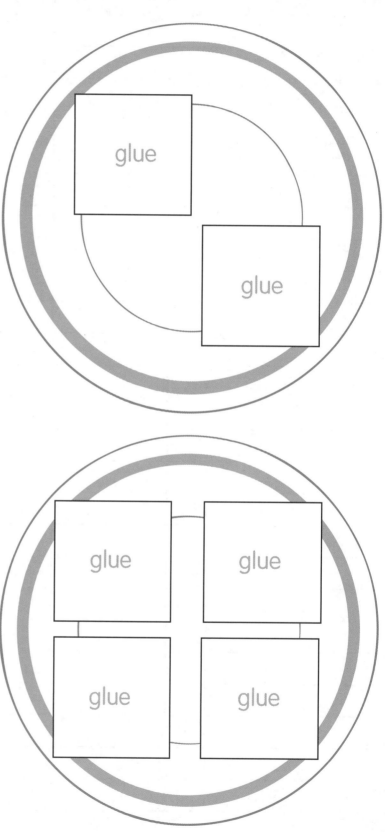

Objective:
Student sorts and classifies pictured objects.

Materials:
Mat, p. 161

Picture Cards, p. 163

Class Checklist, p. 165

Activity Sheet, p. 166

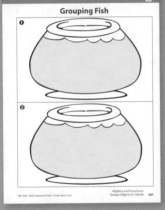

Student Task

Say:

> Today you will put fish into two groups.

Place the picture cards faceup on the table in random order. Place the mat in front of the student. Say:

> Let's begin. Make two groups of fish. Put all the fish that are the same in one fishbowl.

Student groups the fish. Record the response on the class checklist in the section labeled **Groups the Fish**. The student may group the fish in at least two ways—according to category (fish and sea horses) or according to color (orange fish and purple fish).

Then point to each fishbowl and say:

> What is the same about these fish?

Record the student's responses on the class checklist in the section labeled **Classifies the Fish.** Accept reasonable and logical classifications.

Grouping Fish

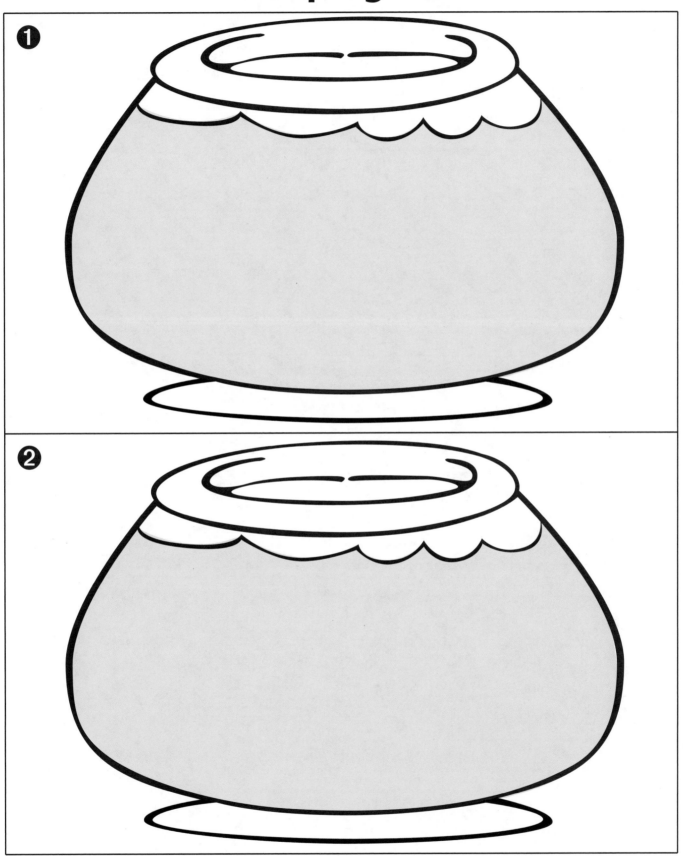

1

2

Algebra and Functions
Groups Objects to Classify **161**

Groups Objects to Classify
Algebra and Functions

EMC 3025 • © Evan-Moor Corp.

Groups Objects to Classify
Algebra and Functions

EMC 3025
© Evan-Moor Corp.

Groups Objects to Classify
Algebra and Functions

EMC 3025
© Evan-Moor Corp.

Groups Objects to Classify
Algebra and Functions

EMC 3025
© Evan-Moor Corp.

Groups Objects to Classify
Algebra and Functions

EMC 3025
© Evan-Moor Corp.

Groups Objects to Classify
Algebra and Functions

EMC 3025
© Evan-Moor Corp.

Groups Objects to Classify
Algebra and Functions

EMC 3025
© Evan-Moor Corp.

Groups Objects to Classify
Algebra and Functions

EMC 3025
© Evan-Moor Corp.

Groups Objects to Classify
Algebra and Functions

EMC 3025
© Evan-Moor Corp.

Groups Objects to Classify
Algebra and Functions

EMC 3025
© Evan-Moor Corp.

Groups Objects to Classify
Algebra and Functions

EMC 3025
© Evan-Moor Corp.

Groups Objects to Classify

Class Checklist		**Key:**	+ correct response	− incorrect response	● self-corrected

Name	Date	Groups the Fish	Classifies the Fish	Notes

Name _____

Happy Bugs

Cut out the bugs.
Group the bugs that are the same.
Glue.

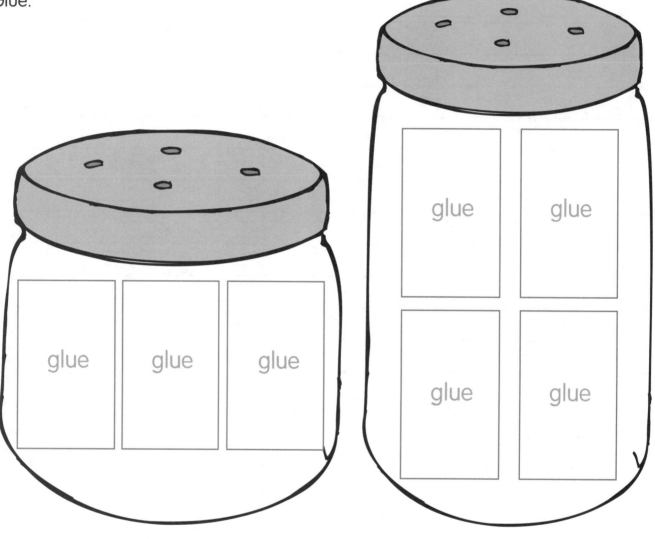

Discriminates Like and Unlike Objects

Objective:
Student determines which pictured object does not belong to a given set.

Materials:
Mat, p. 169

Class Checklist, p. 171

Activity Sheet, p. 172

Blank sheet of paper

Student Task

Say:

> Today you will look at pictures. You will tell me which picture does <u>not</u> belong.

Place the mat in front of the student. Cover all of the rows with a blank sheet of paper except for row 1. Say:

> Let's begin. Look at row 1. Point to what does <u>not</u> belong. Then tell me why it doesn't belong.

Student points to the unlike object. Record the response on the class checklist. You need not record the student's reason for choosing the unlike object, unless it gives insight into the response.

Move the paper down the mat to reveal row 2. Say:

> Look at row 2. Point to what does <u>not</u> belong. Then tell me why it doesn't belong.

Record the response. Then move the paper to reveal row 3. Say:

> Look at row 3. Point to what does <u>not</u> belong. Then tell me why it doesn't belong.

Record the response.

Does Not Belong

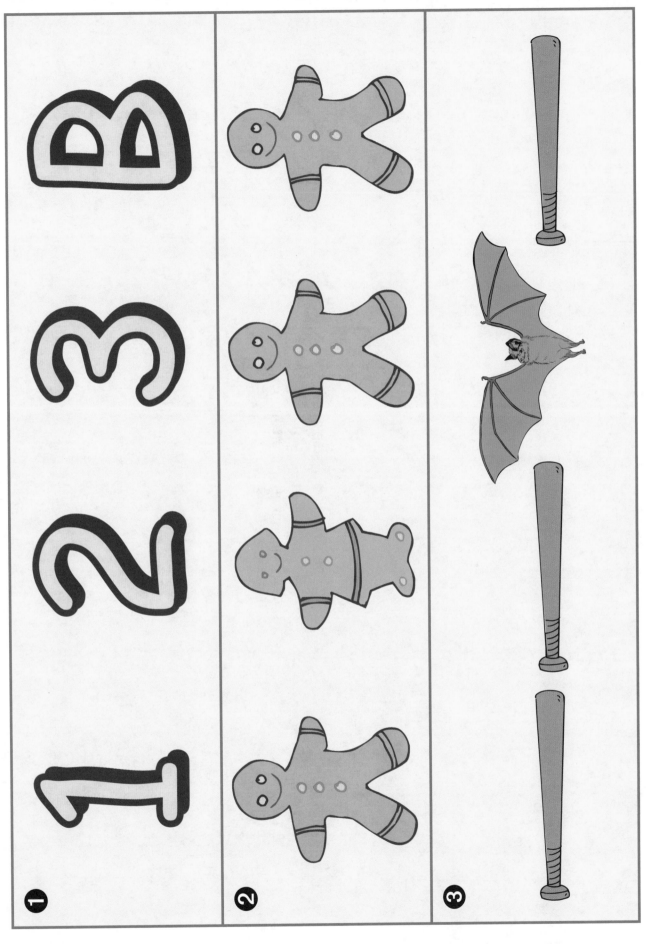

1 B 3 2 1

2

3

Discriminates Like and Unlike Objects

Class Checklist		Key: + correct response − incorrect response ● self-corrected			
Name	Date	Row 1: B	Row 2: Gingerbread Girl	Row 3: Flying Bat	Notes

Name _____

Make an X

What does <u>not</u> belong? Make an **X**.

❶
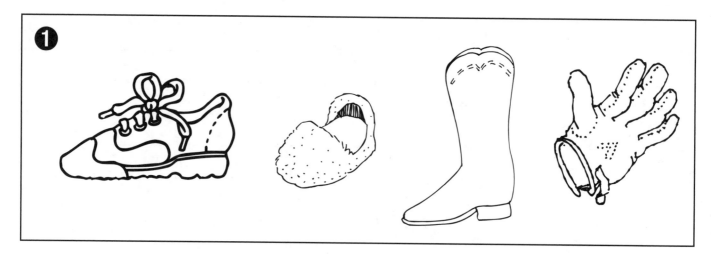

❷

3 A 4 2

❸

Answer Key

Page 16

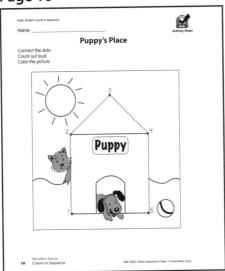

Page 24

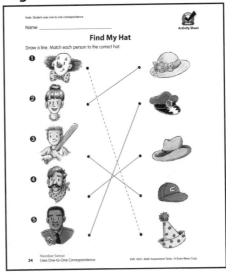

Page 38

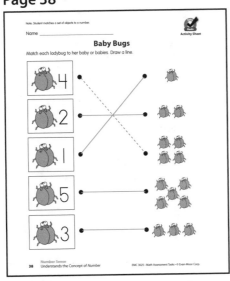

Page 44

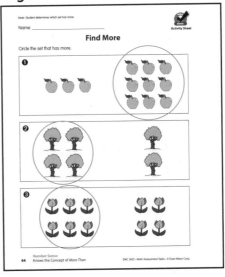

Page 50

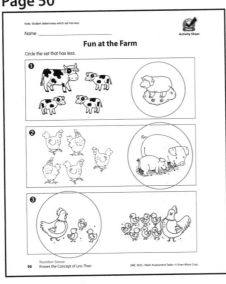

Page 56

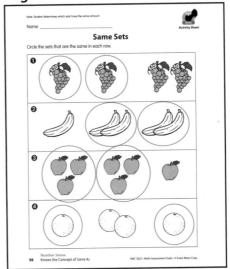

Page 62

Page 70

Page 78

Note: Student adds one more.

Name _____

Activity Sheet

One More

❶ Draw 1 more bone.

Circle how many bones.   1   2   ③

❷ Draw one more ball.

Circle how many balls.   3   ④   5

❸ Draw 1 more house.

Circle how many houses.   ②   3   4

Page 84

Note: Student subtracts concrete objects.

Name _____

Activity Sheet

Pick the Flowers

How many are left?
Circle the number.

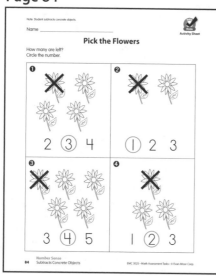

❶   2   ③   4

❷   ①   2   3

❸   3   ④   5

❹   1   ②   3

Page 92

Note: Student recognizes shapes.

Name _____

Activity Sheet

Color the Shapes

blue   green   brown   red

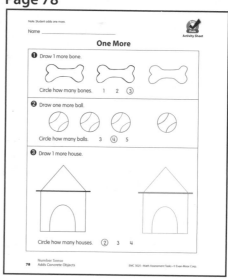

Page 100

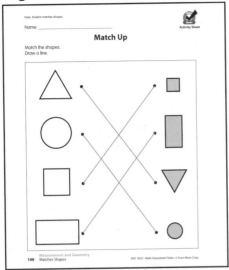

Page 108

Page 114

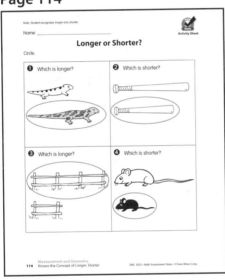

Page 122

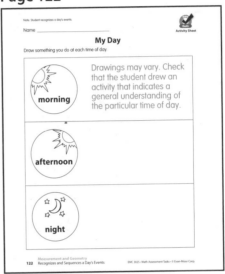

Page 130

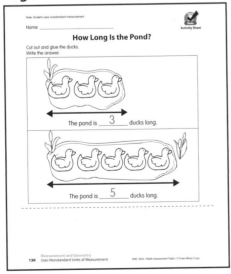

Page 138

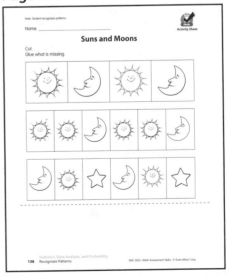

Page 144

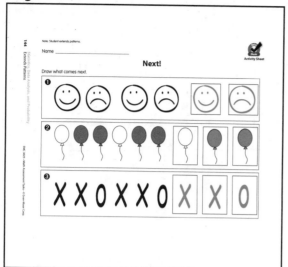

Page 150

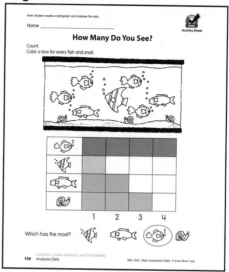

Page 158

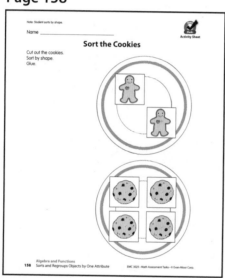

Page 166

Page 172

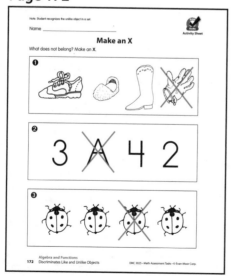